Remember THE WORDS

WHY AND HOW TO MAKE SCRIPTURE MEMORY A WAY OF LIFE

by Dakota Lynch

Remember the Words: Why and How to Make Scripture Memory a Way of Life

ISBN: 979-8-89074-231-5

Scripture Memory Fellowship International
scripturememory.com
888.569.2560 • contact@scripturememory.com • P.O. Box 550232 • Dallas, TX 75355

"Remember the words of the Lord Jesus..."

Acts 20:35

Table of Contents

Introduction

> **He made streams come out of the rock and caused waters to flow down like rivers.**
> **Psalm 78:16**

Throughout Scripture, we learn that God always provides for His people (Phil. 4:19). This provision sometimes comes from unlikely sources—such as food-bearing ravens, stone-slinging shepherds, and water-spewing rocks (1 Kgs. 17:1-6; 1 Sam. 17:50; Num. 20:7-11).

Like fresh water gushing from a rock in the wilderness, Scripture memorization renewed my strength during the most challenging season of my life. My parents divorced when I was 14, leaving me hurt, confused, and mostly alone in my new hometown. At first, memorizing Scripture resembled a rock: dry, boring, and heavy. Yet in time, I saw the water beginning to flow into the most barren parts of my heart. I can now say with the psalmist, "If your law had not been my delight, I would have perished in my affliction" (Psa. 119:92).

Unfortunately, Scripture memorization shares another similarity with water flowing from a rock: it's highly unusual. In today's culture, telling someone you memorize Scripture is like saying you own a pet otter. But things haven't always been that way. For centuries, Christians viewed memorizing Scripture as a way of life. Knowing God's Word wasn't an unusual rock in the wilderness; it was a normal part of the landscape, much like the "ancient landmark" of Proverbs 22:28. Yet despite Solomon's warning, most modern Christians have moved this landmark to the sidelines of their lives. The age-old conviction that God's Word belongs in our hearts has been replaced by the idea that we can simply carry it in our pockets and store it on our shelves.

As you survey your collection of study Bibles, pocket Bibles, audio Bibles, parallel Bibles, and chronological Bibles, it's tempting to conclude that memorizing Scripture is a relic of bygone days when God's Word was less accessible. Is memorizing Bible verses really a critical component of the Christian life? Or, is it the spiritual equivalent of running a marathon—a beneficial exercise for those who are interested, but something the rest of us can opt out of with no shame?

The answer to these questions is found in Psalm 1. In this familiar passage, David describes the man of God as "a tree planted by streams of water that yields its fruit in its season, and its leaf does not wither. In all that he does, he prospers" (vs. 3).

How do we reach this level of spiritual health? The answer is found in verse two: "his delight is in the law of the LORD, and on his law he meditates day and night." Clearly, the psalmist viewed the internalization of Scripture as a prerequisite to a vibrant, fruitful walk with God.

Tragically, most of us find it easier to quote our favorite movies than to remember the words of Jesus—as if we could truly follow Christ without knowing what He said. Meanwhile, studies show that two-thirds of young people who grow up in church will leave between the ages of 18 and 22.[1] It shouldn't be surprising that people who don't know the Bible are more likely to walk away from the faith. After all, "faith comes from hearing, and hearing through the word of Christ" (Rom. 10:17).

This booklet is not an exhaustive manual on proper memorization techniques.[2] Instead, consider it your launching pad into a life where memorizing Scripture is a normal part of your Christian walk. You'll find plenty of practical tips to help you get started, but much of the "how" will be left up to you. After all, the biggest obstacle you'll encounter in your ongoing memorization of Scripture is not a lack of resources but a lack of motivation. Being fully persuaded that God's

---

1 "Reasons 18- to 22-Year-Olds Drop Out of Church," Lifeway Research, Accessed May 31, 2023, https://research.lifeway.com/2007/08/07/reasons-18-to-22-year-olds-drop-out-of-church/.

2 Consider reading *How to Memorize the Bible* by William Evans, *Warriors of the Word* by Aaron and Emily House, and *An Approach to Extended Memorization of Scripture* by Andrew Davis.

Word deserves a lasting place in your heart will take you much further than installing the right Bible memory app.

The ultimate goal of this book is to help you make Deuteronomy 30:14 a reality: "But the word is very near you. It is in your mouth and in your heart, so that you can do it." The following chapters don't contain a secret formula that makes Scripture memory an effortless exercise. Instead, you'll find the encouragement and practical tools you need to hide God's Word in your heart successfully. When it comes to memorizing Scripture, you'll find that while many things are easier, few things are more worthwhile.

NOTES:

_____

_____

_____

_____

> How sweet are your words to my taste, sweeter than honey to my mouth!
> Psalm 119:103

Myth #1: Memorizing Scripture is for people with excellent memories.

Perhaps the most common Scripture memory myth is that hiding God's Word in your heart requires an excellent memory—or at least a memory that's better than yours.

Even if you have a terrible memory, that only heightens the importance of memorizing Scripture! If that seems counterintuitive, think of it this way: people who are out of shape benefit from physical exercise much more than those who are naturally athletic. If you're prone to forgetting the words of Scripture, taking time to refill your mind with biblical truth will be especially worthwhile.

It's also helpful to realize that your memory is probably a lot better than you think it is. How many song lyrics do you know? How many movie lines can you quote? How many players can you name from your favorite sports team? As a new Christian, the idea that I was somehow disadvantaged in my ability to memorize Scripture nearly kept me from ever trying. Then, I was challenged by these words from David Nasser:

> *I hear people whine, "I can't memorize verses from the Bible. It's too hard!" That's ridiculous. These same people know every song on their favorite CD, and I know a couple of guys who can recite the entire dialogue from* The Three Amigos *word for word! The first thing I want you to realize is: yes, you* can *memorize verses from the Bible!* [1]

---

1   David Nasser, *A Call to Die* (Baxter Press, 2000), 18.

These words helped me realize that I didn't have a bad memory; I had a *neglected* memory. I was quite proficient at retaining song lyrics, movie lines, and sports stats. Was this because batting averages are inherently easier to memorize than Bible verses? Or, did the contents of my memory simply reflect my flawed priorities? The answer was clear: I had a perfectly functional memory, but I had never intentionally filled it with God's Word.

After a few weeks of memorizing Scripture, two things became clear:

1. **Memorizing Scripture isn't any harder than other types of memorization.** I know the lines to my favorite movies because I've watched them again and again, yet I thought memorizing Scripture should happen by osmosis. I claimed to be bad at memorizing Scripture when, in fact, I had spent very little time trying.

2. **Memorizing Scripture is indescribably worthwhile.** I started memorizing Scripture because I thought it was my Christian duty. But within only a few months, the seeds of Scripture planted in my heart started to sprout and bear fruit in obvious and not-so-obvious ways. My prayer life, thought life, and day-to-day conversations were all impacted by the truth of Scripture. I realized that Bible verses encouraging us to memorize Scripture (e.g. Psa. 119:11; Deut. 6:6) aren't there to make the Christian life unnecessarily difficult. In fact, the opposite is true: knowing and meditating on Scripture is the key to spiritual prosperity and "good success" (Josh. 1:8).

Over the years, I've met Christians who know hundreds or even thousands of Bible verses by heart. The people who are most successful in this discipline—like my friend Aaron who memorized the entire New Testament—don't have above-average memories. Instead, they have above-average determination. The reason Aaron can recite the book of Romans isn't that he has a photographic memory; it's that he spent hundreds of hours practicing those verses when he could have been watching TV.

> **"The busier you are, the more you need God's Word."**

Myth #2: Memorizing Scripture is for people with lots of free time.

Just as most people believe they have below-average memories, many of us think we are too busy to memorize Scripture. Things like media, work, school, and parenting crowd our schedules and seemingly leave no room for systematic memorization of Scripture.

The problem with this excuse is that we always make time for what we value most. How much time do you spend on Facebook, Instagram, and YouTube? Doomscrolling the news? Following your favorite sports team or politicians? According to a 2022 study, most adults average 147 minutes per day on social media.[2]

In the words of John Piper, "One of the great uses of Twitter and Facebook will be to prove at the Last Day that prayerlessness was not from lack of time."[3] Similarly, we can't claim busyness as an excuse for not memorizing Scripture while we faithfully make time for social media, Netflix, and our favorite hobbies. Are we guilty of giving a tithe of our time to our phone screens while giving God the crumbs that fall from the table of our ever-busy lives?

Even if you somehow manage to avoid these common timewasters, resist the temptation to place God's Word on the back burner until things settle down. In the words of Max Barnett,

2   "Daily Time Spent on Social Networking by Internet Users Worldwide from 2012 to 2022," Statista, Accessed May 30, 2023, https://www.statista.com/statistics/433871/daily-social-media-usage-worldwide/.

3   John Piper, Twitter Post, October 20, 2009, 4:02 PM, Accessed May 30, 2023, https://twitter.com/johnpiper/status/5027319857.

If you truly are too busy [to memorize], then maybe you are busier than God intended for you to be. Maybe you need to seriously evaluate the way you use your time. The problem is usually not a lack of time but a lack of heart. Ask God to help you deal with your heart and find some time to memorize His Word.[4]

The busier you are, the more you need God's Word. This is true for the same reason that a seatbelt becomes more important at high speeds. Is your life filled with daily decisions and responsibilities? If so, knowing Scripture by heart is crucial. "For the LORD gives wisdom; from his mouth come knowledge and understanding" (Prov. 2:6).

Sometimes, setting aside good things is necessary to make time for the best things.

Myth #3: Memorizing Scripture isn't necessary in the digital age.

An unfortunate side effect of the digital age is that we often treat our smartphones as a substitute for knowing God's Word personally. Memorizing Scripture, once treated as an indispensable spiritual discipline, now appears as the spiritual equivalent of a fax machine: outdated, inferior, and probably unnecessary. Why take time to memorize a verse that's never more than a few clicks away?

As we ponder this question, it's worth remembering that Scripture memory has been a normal part of the Christian life throughout church history.[5] The saints of old believed that following Christ began with knowing what He said. The notion that we can outsource this component of discipleship to Google or AI represents a clear departure from the age-old belief that God's Word belongs in our

4   Max D. Barnett, *The Value of Memorizing Scripture* (The Real Purpose of Life Publications, 2016), 17.

5   Thomas Meyer, *The Memorization Study Bible* (New Leaf Press: 2020), 477.

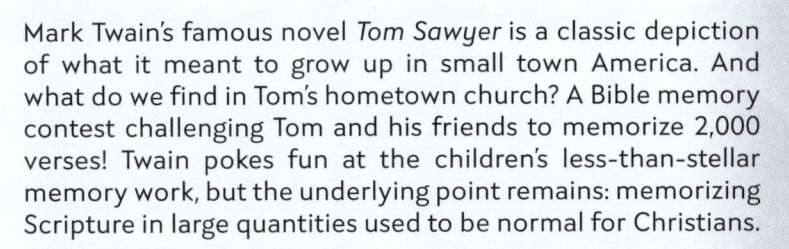

> **"The digital age hasn't eliminated the need to memorize Scripture. It has heightened it!"**

hearts (not just our pockets). Before moving "the ancient landmark that your fathers have set" (Prov. 22:28), it's important to pause and consider the consequences.

Mark Twain's famous novel *Tom Sawyer* is a classic depiction of what it meant to grow up in small town America. And what do we find in Tom's hometown church? A Bible memory contest challenging Tom and his friends to memorize 2,000 verses! Twain pokes fun at the children's less-than-stellar memory work, but the underlying point remains: memorizing Scripture in large quantities used to be normal for Christians.

It would be convenient if modern technology eliminated the need for Scripture memory. But has our culture's increased smartphone usage coincided with increased love for God and His Word? Has the proliferation of Bible apps slowed the spread of heresy? Has our unprecedented access to Scripture produced unprecedented revival and spiritual growth?

The proof is in the pudding. We've had enough time to see whether Google and Bible apps are viable substitutes for knowing God's Word personally. Clearly, they are not. We have a wealth of biblical knowledge at our fingertips, and yet most of it stays there, never making it into our minds and hearts.

The following statistics paint a grim picture of just how widespread biblical illiteracy has become:

• Only 20% of Americans have ever read the whole Bible.[6]

• 3% of teens read the Bible every day.[7]

---

6   "Lifeway Research: Americans Are Fond of the Bible, Don't Actually Read It," Lifeway Research, Accessed May 30, 2023, https://research.lifeway.com/2017/04/25/lifeway-research-americans-are-fond-of-the-bible-dont-actually-read-it/.

7   "9 Surprising Facts About Teens and the Bible," Lifeway Research, Accessed May 30, 2023, https://research.lifeway.com/2016/09/07/9-surprising-facts-about-teens-and-the-bible/.

• Less than half of adults can name all four Gospels.[8]

More than ever, America is facing a famine. This is "not a famine of bread, nor a thirst for water, but of hearing the words of the LORD" (Amos 8:11). Notice Amos describes a very specific famine: it's not a famine of *having* God's Word, but a famine of *hearing* God's Word! In an age when Americans spend $500 million on Bibles annually, it's clear that we don't face a famine of having physical copies of Scripture. But it's increasingly apparent that a famine of hearing has swept the land—especially when you consider that most high school seniors think Sodom and Gomorrah were husband and wife![9]

If having God's Word on our smartphones was a viable substitute for knowing Scripture by heart, we could expect this generation to be among the godliest in history. Instead, we see widespread apostasy and staggering levels of biblical illiteracy.

The digital age hasn't eliminated the need to memorize Scripture. It has heightened it! With news and social media constantly at our fingertips, the world has a direct line to our eyes and ears. Properly processing this endless stream of headlines, advertisements, memes, debates, and temptation requires more than installing God's Word on your phone; we need it in our hearts (Psa. 119:9).

NOTES:

_____

_____

8   "5 Facts on how Americans View the Bible and Other Religious Texts," Pew Research Center, Accessed May 30, 2023, https://www.pewresearch.org/short-reads/2017/04/14/5-facts-on-how-americans-view-the-bible-and-other-religious-texts/.

9   Dr. R. Albert Mohler, "The Scandal of Biblical Illiteracy," Answers in Genesis, Accessed May 30, 2023, https://answersingenesis.org/christianity/scandal-biblical-illiteracy/.

THE THREE W'S OF MEMORIZING SCRIPTURE
Chapter 2

> For the word of God is living and active, sharper than any two-edged sword, piercing to the division of soul and of spirit, of joints and of marrow, and discerning the thoughts and intentions of the heart.
> **Hebrews 4:12**

Everyone memorizes differently. Visual learners may like flashcards, while others prefer audio tools such as voice recorders and Scripture songs. Because everyone has a different learning style, providing a one-size-fits-all solution to memorizing Scripture is impossible. What works well for me may be completely unhelpful to you, and vice versa.

Whether you're an auditory learner, a visual learner, or somewhere in between, The Three W's of Memorizing Scripture will help you get started and stay on track for the long haul.

The First W: What will you memorize?

> The law of your mouth is better to me than thousands of gold and silver pieces.
> **Psalm 119:72**

Selecting a passage of Scripture to memorize is a critical first step. You may be convinced that you need to start memorizing in a general sense, but tangible progress rarely happens apart from specific goals. As the saying goes, "If you aim at nothing, you'll hit it."

Thankfully, this step is the easiest. You might decide to memorize Psalm 23, the Beatitudes, or the Romans Road. A great option for new memorizers is *The Classics: 100*

> ## "Tangible progress rarely happens apart from specific goals."

Bible Verses Everyone Should Know by Scripture Memory Fellowship.[1]

Should you memorize whole chapters or topically?

As you decide what to memorize, you might wonder whether to memorize whole chapters or by topic. Each approach has its benefits, and you should plan to do some of both in the coming years.

If you're a new memorizer, consider memorizing Scripture topically at first. What does the Bible say about God and His work in Creation? What does it teach us about how to please Him in our thoughts, words, and actions? What verses should we know about the person and work of Jesus Christ? What promises of God should we take with us in preparation for our next encounter with temptation or despair? Having a storehouse of memorized Scripture on each of these questions is invaluable, yet no one chapter or book of the Bible answers them all.

Some people object that memorizing topically is a recipe for misunderstanding the Bible and taking verses out of context. This point isn't without merit, but Jesus Himself demonstrated that it's possible to recite Scripture topically without taking it out of context (Matt. 4:4, 7, 10). The apostle Paul's writings are also filled with short, relevant quotes from the Old Testament (Rom. 12:20, 14:11; 1 Cor. 2:16; Gal. 3:13; Eph. 4:8, etc.).

Daily conversations usually don't call for a complete recitation of James 1. When a friend faces an uphill battle, verses 2-3

---

1   Available at scripturememory.com/classics

may be sufficient: "Count it all joy, my brothers, when you meet trials of various kinds, for you know that the testing of your faith produces steadfastness."

Memorizing topically involves some risk of misapplying Scripture, but this danger persists even when memorizing longer passages. For example, suppose a new believer begins her Scripture memory journey by learning the book of James. Correctly interpreting James' emphasis on works would be difficult without a well-balanced knowledge of other Scripture, such as Romans 3-4 and Ephesians 2:8-9.

By beginning with topical memorization, you'll establish a broad knowledge of the Bible that equips you to interpret Scripture with Scripture and rightly divide "the word of truth" (2 Tim. 2:15).

When deciding what to memorize, remember that "all Scripture is breathed out by God" (2 Tim. 3:16). This takes the stress out of choosing what to memorize. If memorizing your favorite psalm sounds more appealing than memorizing topically, go for it! The fact that you're memorizing Scripture is far more important than what particular passage you choose to memorize. As Andrew Davis writes,

> When Judgment Day comes, we will regret the waste of a single moment not used for the glory of Christ. We will, however, not regret one moment we spent diligently studying God's Word and hiding it in our heart. We will only wish we'd spent more time doing this.[2]

Once you decide what to memorize, use the space on the next page to write down your new goal. Having a specific chapter or set of verses to work on will take you much further than simply believing you should memorize Scripture in general. This seemingly small step represents a giant leap forward in your Scripture memory journey.

---

2   Andrew Davis, *An Approach to Extended Memorization of Scripture*, Scripture Memory Fellowship, Accessed May 30, 2023, https://scripturememory.com/downloadables/andrewdavis.pdf.

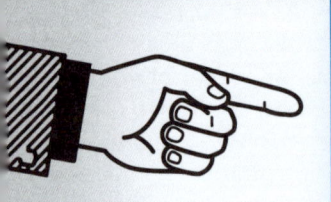

> ## "Choose a target completion date that's both challenging and realistic."

What specific passage(s) of Scripture have you chosen to memorize?

_____

_____

The Second W: When Will You Finish?

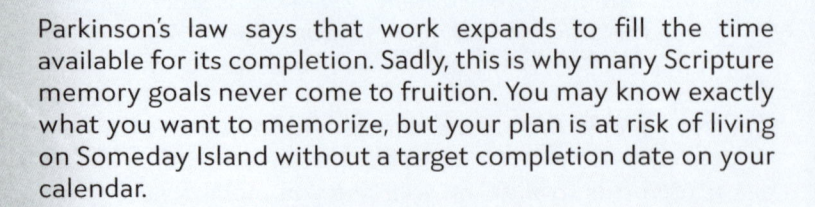

Commit your work to the LORD, and your plans will be established.
Proverbs 16:3

Parkinson's law says that work expands to fill the time available for its completion. Sadly, this is why many Scripture memory goals never come to fruition. You may know exactly what you want to memorize, but your plan is at risk of living on Someday Island without a target completion date on your calendar.

Choose a target completion date that's both challenging and realistic. If you're a new memorizer, think of it like joining a gym: starting with the heaviest weights is probably unwise. At the same time, if you reach your goal without breaking a sweat, it's time to step it up a notch. Your Scripture memory goal should strike the same balance. Memorizing Hebrews by the end of next month would represent very heavy lifting, but giving yourself six months to learn the Beatitudes represents the opposite extreme.

Before deciding when you'll finish, it's helpful to determine how many verses you plan to memorize each week. Two or three verses per week is a reasonable goal for most new memorizers. As you exercise your memory, you'll likely find that this number can increase.

I typically average a few verses per week in my own memorization, but there have been occasional bursts of 10-20 verses in a single day. This usually happens when I'm in the home stretch of memorizing a particular set of verses and am eager to cross the finish line.

Of course, memorizing 20 verses in an afternoon doesn't happen often. This isn't a realistic goal for new memorizers or even a sustainable pace for experienced memorizers. I share this example only to demonstrate the power of human memory. Remember, I was so convinced my memory was below average that I nearly missed out on the joy of memorizing Scripture. Learning two verses per week may seem overwhelming now, but you'll find that your memory is like a muscle: the more you exercise it, the stronger it becomes.

After deciding how many verses you will memorize each week, choosing a target completion date is easy. Are you planning to memorize 10 verses from the Romans Road plan of salvation?[3] If so, a pace of two verses per week means your target completion date should be in five weeks.

If your completion date is more than two or three months away, consider splitting your memory goal into more manageable chunks. Rather than deciding when you'll finish the entire Sermon on the Mount, mark your calendar for when you'll recite Matthew 5. Once you reach that checkpoint, move on to the next chapter with a fresh deadline.

---

3   You can download the Romans Road verses at verselocker.com/romansroad.

> ## "Achieving uncommon results requires uncommon intentionality."

This piecemeal approach accomplishes two things:

1. **It prevents discouragement.** When your goal is to climb Mount Everest, nothing is more disheartening than looking up and seeing how much farther you have to go. This is especially true in seasons when an unexpected illness or travel causes you to fall behind in your memory work. By contrast, "a desire fulfilled is sweet to the soul" (Prov. 13:19). Short-term goals provide more frequent opportunities for this sort of celebration, keeping you motivated and on track.

2. **It provides opportunities for adjustment.** Since memorizing gets easier with practice, you might hit your stride and find that you can memorize five verses per week in the same amount of time it used to take you to learn two. Or, you might discover a need to slow down and allow more time for review. When your target completion date is never more than two or three months away, you'll have regular opportunities to make these adjustments.

At this point, it might seem like The Three W's of Memorizing Scripture are incredibly legalistic. Is it really necessary to map out your memory work, commit to a weekly pace, and set a target completion date? If your goal is to halfway know a small handful of Bible verses, perhaps not. But if you're ready to swim against the current of biblical illiteracy and strengthen your grip on "the sword of the Spirit" (Eph. 6:17), then be prepared to take the path less traveled. It's true that most people don't make Scripture memory this complicated.

It's also true that most Americans can't name even five of the Ten Commandments.[4]

When it comes to memorizing Scripture, achieving uncommon results requires uncommon intentionality. So after deciding what you will memorize, choose a target completion date to help you stay on track.

When will you finish memorizing your chosen passage(s)?

_____

_____

4   Dr. R. Albert Mohler, "The Scandal of Biblical Illiteracy," Answers in Genesis, Accessed May 30, 2023, https://answersingenesis.org/christianity/scandal-biblical-illiteracy/.

The Third W: Who will hear you recite?

> **Iron sharpens iron, and one man sharpens another.**
> **Proverbs 27:17**

This is the hard one. Nobody likes accountability, but we all need it. In fact, research shows that accountability drastically increases the odds of achieving your goals. Your likelihood of success is:

- 10% if you have a specific **idea or goal**

- 25% if you consciously **decide** to do it

- 40% if you decide **when** you will do it

- 50% if you plan **how** you will do it

- 65% if you **commit to someone else** that you will do it

- 95% if you have a specific **accountability appointment** with that person[5]

If you picked up this book looking for the secret to memorizing Scripture, here it is! When you plan to memorize a specific set of verses and then share that plan with someone to whom you'll recite regularly, you're virtually guaranteed to succeed! Skipping the accountability component may be tempting, but you'll be much less likely to cross the finish line.

The good news is that accountability doesn't have to be awkward. Don't think of it as a weekly exam. Instead, view it as a weekly opportunity to share God's Word. After reciting, "encourage one another and build one another up" by discussing the verses you've recited and how to apply them (1 Thess. 5:11).

On a practical note, it's important to select a hearer who will truly hold you accountable and stir you up "to love and good works" (Heb. 10:24). Ideally, this accountability should come

5 "Reaching My Health Goals," Lifemed Clinic, Accessed May 30, 2023, https://lifemedclinic.org/reaching-my-health-goals/.

from someone outside your home. Although your family members may be willing, they are generally most lenient when you need a push.

If possible, you should also select a hearer who is a fellow Scripture memorizer. Consider the words of Solomon in Ecclesiastes 4:9-10:

> *Two are better than one, because they have a good reward for their toil. For if they fall, one will lift up his fellow. But woe to him who is alone when he falls and has not another to lift him up!*

If your accountability comes from someone who isn't memorizing Scripture also, it may be harder to get up when you fall down. This is true for the same reason you wouldn't ask a couch potato to help you train for a marathon. You need someone who shares your values, both intellectually and experientially.

> "Accountability drastically increases the odds of achieving your goals."

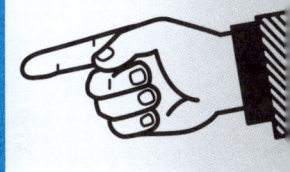

But what if you don't know any other Scripture memorizers? What if you are the only one in your family or church who actively memorizes God's Word? In that case, remember that fellow memorizers may be hiding in plain sight. My friend Daniel has faithfully memorized Scripture for years but seldom talks about it. For him, this spiritual discipline is a very personal and private part of his walk with God. Before concluding that you are the only Christian within 50 miles who cares about memorizing Scripture, ask a few mature believers in your church if they memorize or would be willing to start. You might be surprised by their answers!

If you simply cannot find a fellow memorizer to hear your verses, consider reciting to an unbeliever instead. Perhaps you've been looking for an opportunity to share the gospel with your unsaved coworkers or neighbors. What better way to do so than by inviting them to follow along as you recite Ephesians 2? They may not hold you accountable with the same zeal as a fellow believer, but knowing God may use your recitations to draw them to saving faith will provide significant motivation.

If accountability feels unnatural and unnecessary, remember that your goal isn't just to memorize Scripture for the next few weeks. It's to make Scripture memory a new way of life! You may not need accountability this week when the fire of self-motivation is burning brightly, but let's face it: you won't always feel like memorizing Scripture (more on that in chapter eight). There will be seasons when busyness crowds your schedule and distractions crowd your thoughts. Or, you might find that the newness of memorizing Scripture simply wears off over time, leaving you with a fraction of the zeal you feel today.

If you're convinced that memorizing Scripture is worth prioritizing over the long haul, take steps now to ensure your goals become a reality. Like a seatbelt, accountability provides stability when you encounter unexpected obstacles in life. And like a seatbelt, you should proactively use it even when the road ahead seems clear.

Who will be your hearer, and how often will this person hear you recite?

_____

_____

_____

> I will never forget your precepts, for by them you
> have given me life.
> Psalm 119:93

Once you've identified what you will memorize, when you will finish, and who will hear you recite, you're ready to begin memorizing Scripture! This chapter contains seven tried-and-true principles to help you make Scripture memory a consistent and enjoyable part of daily life.

Identify your learning style.

Memorizing Scripture never comes effortlessly, but you can streamline the process by identifying your unique learning style. In other words, find out which memory techniques work best for you. Are you a visual learner? If so, try writing your verses on index cards with the Scripture text on one side and the reference on the back. If you're an auditory learner, use an audio Bible or your smartphone's voice recorder to listen to your verses on a loop. Kinesthetic learners might find it easier to memorize while pacing the floor, whereas others memorize best in an easy chair.

Don't be surprised if it takes several weeks to identify your unique learning style. After all, rote memorization is a neglected discipline in our culture. A person who never exercises probably won't know what type of runner he is until he has logged a few dozen miles. Unless you've been exercising your "memory muscle" elsewhere, it might take a while to identify the methods that work well for you.

During your first few weeks of memorizing, try everything. Yes, *everything*. As Dr. Seuss would say, try memorizing here and there. Try memorizing everywhere! Try memorizing in a house, with a mouse, in the rain, on a train, in a box, or with a fox (okay, maybe not with a fox). Memorize Scripture in a variety of ways, then stick with the most effective methods.

> # "Spending 10 minutes per day on your verses is better than spending an hour on them every Saturday."

Find your Scripture memory time and place.

Forming new habits can be difficult. One way to help Scripture memory become a consistent part of your daily life is to use what James Clear calls habit stacking.[1] Rather than building a new habit from scratch, build it upon the foundation of another habit you have already mastered. Think of something you do every day, like pouring your coffee or taking off your shoes, and make that your daily cue to memorize.

- "After I pour my coffee, I will spend five minutes reviewing my verses for the week."

- "After I take off my shoes in the evening, I will recite two verses from memory."

- "After my shower, I will focus on memorizing something new."

Rather than deciding 365 times per year whether you'll memorize Scripture, determine in advance when and where it's going to happen.

Remember that the goal isn't to become a memory champion; it's to make Scripture memory a consistent part of your day. Spending 10 minutes per day on your verses is better than spending an hour on them every Saturday. "Instead of trying to engineer a perfect habit from the start, do the easy thing

---

1   James Clear, *Atomic Habits* (Cornerstone press, 2022), 72.

on a more consistent basis. You have to standardize before you can optimize."[2]

>
> ## "When it comes to memorizing Scripture, distractions are your worst enemy."

Eliminate distractions.

Most people take pride in their ability to multitask. You might be able to talk on the phone, check your email, and walk the dog simultaneously. But when it comes to memorizing Scripture, distractions are your worst enemy. Memorization requires your undivided attention. So turn off the television, silence your cell phone, and find a quiet place to focus exclusively on God's Word. As William Evans writes, "Attention is fixity of thought. The ability to fix your thought on what you desire to memorize is the first essential principle in the training of the memory."[3]

A word of warning: eliminating distractions may prove harder than it sounds. Our lives are filled with constant alerts, notifications, and messages. Silencing our devices sounds easy enough, but the modern brain is so accustomed to distractions that it often prefers them. "[T]he constant shifting of our attention when we're online may make our brains more nimble when it comes to multitasking, but improving our ability to multitask actually hampers our ability to think deeply and creatively."[4]

---

2   Ibid., 163.

3   William Evans, *How to Memorize the Bible* (CrossReach Publications, 2016), 26.

4   Nicholas Carr, *The Shallows* (Atlantic Books, 2020), 140.

"The good news is that you can train your brain."

Even if you're completely alone in an empty room, be prepared for your brain to resist the unfamiliar exercise of rote memorization. You've spent years training your brain to jump from one thought or task to the next. Asking it to spend 15 minutes focused on the same 20 words represents a significant change of pace. After a few moments of memorizing, you'll notice a bit of trash on the floor. After throwing it away, you'll see that the trash can is full. Emptying the trash reminds you that you need to add trash bags to your shopping list, which reminds you that you didn't finish meal planning for next week. Your first 15 minutes of memorizing Scripture might take 30 minutes to accomplish.

The good news is that you can train your brain. Believe it or not, the fact that we are so easily distracted is evidence of our brains' adaptability. In less than a century, we've gone from reading novels and newspapers to skimming blog posts and scanning the headlines in our news feed. For our grandparents, deep reading and rote memorization were a way of life. For us, screens are a way of life. Our proficiency at multi-tasking and speed-reading illustrates just how quickly our brains have adapted to their new environment. Humankind hasn't lost its ability to memorize or think deeply over the last 50 years; we're simply out of practice.

As Nicholas Carr writes,

> Whether I'm online or not, my mind now expects to take in information the way the Net distributes it: in a swiftly moving stream of particles. Once I was a scuba diver in the sea of words. Now I zip along the surface like a guy on a Jet Ski.[5]

---

5   Nicholas Carr, *The Shallows* (Atlantic Books, 2020), 6.

If scuba divers can learn to jet ski, then jet skiers can learn to scuba dive. It just takes time.

Develop a review system.

Memorizing a phone number is easy if you only need to remember it for the next 10 seconds. Your short-term memory can store information quickly, but preserving something in your long-term memory requires time and patience. Just because you recited a verse perfectly doesn't mean you should put it in the "memorized" column just yet.

This is where many new memorizers become discouraged. Imagine a new memorizer reciting Psalm 23 from memory for the first time, then closing his Bible and congratulating himself on a job well done. A week later, he tries to recite it again and can't get past verse one. This isn't a sign that he has defective memory and can't memorize; it's a sign that the verses never made it into long-term memory.

> **"It's better to say a verse every day for 100 days than to say it 100 times in an afternoon."**

When you begin memorizing a new verse, commit to reviewing it daily. It's better to say a verse every day for 100 days than to say it 100 times in an afternoon. As you learn and relearn the same passage again and again, it will eventually establish a home in your long-term memory. By reviewing a verse right before you would otherwise forget it, you're casting a vote for the importance of that memory. You're telling your brain, "Hang onto this; it's important!"

Over time, you'll be able to review a verse less often without forgetting it. After a week or two of daily review, try reviewing it every other day. If that goes well, try reviewing it weekly, then monthly, then quarterly. The goal is to maintain what you've already memorized while still allowing plenty of time to learn new verses.

If keeping track of how often to review your memory verses sounds cumbersome, consider using VerseLocker.[6] SMF's free Bible memory app lets you choose how often you'd like to review each of your verses, and it quizzes you on the verses due for review each day. The app also has several audio and visual tools that optimize the memorization process.

If you'd rather not use digital tools, try writing each of your memory verses on an index card. Store your cards in a small box with dividers for various review intervals: daily, weekly, monthly, etc. Every day, review the verses from the "daily" section. Every Sunday, review the verses in the "weekly" section, and so on.

> ## "Pick a single translation and stick with it."

Pick a translation.

There are more than 100 English translations of the Bible. Yet when it comes to memorization, it's crucial to pick a single translation and stick with it. Word-perfect accuracy is important when memorizing Scripture, yet this becomes a moving target when we encounter different renderings of the same verse in our printed Bible, family devotionals, church services, and Bible apps.

Of course, complete consistency may not be possible. Some churches use one translation in Sunday School, another in the worship service, and yet another for the children's ministry. Translation consistency isn't important enough to warrant changing churches or skipping Sunday School. But whenever possible, do yourself a favor by reading and memorizing from the same translation.

"But how do I know which translation to memorize?" The answer to that question varies from person to person. If you've been reading the ESV or the KJV for the last decade, you probably have a head start memorizing many classic passages like The Lord's Prayer and the Beatitudes. Don't make Scripture memory even harder by abandoning the translation with which you're most familiar.

If you're not already committed to a particular translation, consider these factors as you make your decision:

> ## "Every word in the Bible is there on purpose!"

1: "All Scripture is breathed out by God" (2 Tim. 3:16).

This means that every word in the Bible is there on purpose! Theologians refer to this doctrine as "verbal plenary inspiration." God didn't just inspire the "big ideas" of Scripture; He chose the exact words! That's why it's important to select a literal, word-for-word translation that honors this principle.

By contrast, some translations use a thought-for-thought approach. While no language can be translated 100% word-for-word, choose a literal translation that honors the way God has "breathed out" Scripture "in words not taught by human wisdom but taught by the Spirit" (2 Tim. 3:16; 1 Cor. 2:13).

Thought-for-thought translations may indeed capture the intended meaning of Scripture. But at certain points they are only as accurate as the translators' understanding of

Scripture. If the translators misunderstood what the original text means, so will we. It's much better to translate Scripture word-for-word and leave illumination to the Holy Spirit. "Now we have received not the spirit of the world, but the Spirit who is from God, that we might understand the things freely given us by God" (1 Cor. 2:12).

💡 Visit scripturememory.com/translations for a free Bible translation comparison chart.

2: Modern translations can be updated.

In 2011, one of the most popular translations of the Bible was completely overhauled—much to the dismay of Scripture memorizers who had invested years memorizing from it. Several other translations have published updates since then, usually in an attempt to keep up with the ever-changing English language.

Unfortunately, such updates typically coincide with a complete purge of the previous version of a translation. Since these translations are copyrighted, the copyright holders can (and usually do) require printing companies and even Bible apps to use the updated version. Imagine purchasing a new Bible in five years and discovering that your favorite translation has been quietly replaced with a very different translation bearing the same name!

Of course, you can't prevent a copyrighted translation from being updated. You can, however, research a translation's history and see how frequently and extensively it has been updated. Also, remember that newer translations are more likely to be updated as the translators continue refining their work.

3: Don't stress it.

If you're feeling overwhelmed at the thought of choosing a translation, don't be! There's no one-size-fits-all Bible translation, so don't stress about finding the one translation that's superior to all others. There are many excellent Bible

> **"Choosing a translation shouldn't feel like searching for a diamond in the rough."**

translations out there. Choosing a translation shouldn't feel like searching for a diamond in the rough, yet I have friends who have literally spent years deciding on a translation. After taking time to prayerfully consider the options, make a decision—preferably within a week or two. The testimonies of Bible memorizers around the world make it clear: God's Word is so potent that its sweetness and power shine through all across the broad spectrum of translations!

Get some sleep.

Memorizing anything involves three things: acquisition, consolidation, and recall.

- *Acquisition* is when you first learn something new.

- *Consolidation* is when short-term memories are converted to stable, long-term memories.

- *Recall* is when you can successfully access the memory in the future.[7]

Acquisition and recall happen when you're awake. Consolidation, on the other hand, happens while you sleep. According to Dr. Matthew Walker at the University of California, "We've learned that sleep before learning helps prepare your brain for initial formation of memories. And then, sleep after learning is essential to help save and cement that new information into the architecture of the brain, meaning that you're less likely to forget it."[8]

7 "Sleep and Memory," Division of Sleep Medicine, Accessed June 5, 2023, https://sleep.hms.harvard.edu/education-training/public-education/sleep-and-health-education-program/sleep-health-education-88.

8 "Sleep On It: How Snoozing Strengthens Memories," News in Health, Accessed May 30, 2023, https://newsinhealth.nih.gov/2013/04/sleep-it.

Some memorizers find it easier to remember their verses the next day if they review them right before bedtime. Notre Dame psychologist Jessica Payne writes,

> *Since we found that sleeping soon after learning benefited both types of memory, this means that it would be a good thing to rehearse any information you need to remember just prior to going to bed. In some sense, you may be 'telling' the sleeping brain what to consolidate.*[9]

Just do it!

Planning is important. As Jesus said, "For which of you, desiring to build a tower, does not first sit down and count the cost, whether he has enough to complete it?" (Luke 14:28). Determine what you will memorize and when you'll finish. Find an accountability partner. Choose a translation. Identify the place and time of day that work best for you. Decide on the tools you'll use to aid your memorization. Develop a plan for how you'll review the verses you've memorized. And then, most importantly, start memorizing! Remember: the best athletes spend much more time exercising than they spend researching the best gym shoes.

NOTES:

_____

_____

_____

_____

9 "Sleeping after Processing New Info Most Effective, New Study Shows," Notre Dame News, Accessed May 30, 2023, https://news.nd.edu/news/learning-best-when-you-rest-sleeping-after-processing-new-info-most-effective-new-study-shows/.

> **How sweet are your words to my taste, sweeter than honey to my mouth!**
> **Psalm 119:103**

Most of our time thus far has been spent exploring the general principles of memorization. In this chapter, we'll examine some of the most common Scripture memory tools and methods.

Inevitably, you'll find some of these methods more helpful than others based on your unique learning style. Rather than viewing this chapter as a step-by-step guide to memorizing a Bible verse, view it as a buffet. There's something here for everyone, but that doesn't mean it's all here for you. Feel free to use the resources you find helpful and skip the ones you don't.

Flash Cards

Scripture memorization doesn't have to be complicated, and flashcards are a simple yet effective way to make it happen. When I began memorizing as a teenager, I wrote the text of each memory verse on an index card with the reference (e.g. John 3:16) on the back. I stored my verse cards in two containers: one was marked "learning," and the other was marked "memorized." I reviewed verses in the "learning" box every day, and I reviewed the "memorized" box about once per week.

> **"Scripture memorization doesn't have to be complicated."**

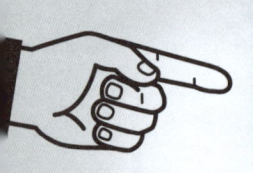

"Technology doesn't have to be a hindrance to your Scripture memory."

An added benefit of using flash cards is that creating them helps solidify God's Word in your memory. Manually writing out each verse may feel painstakingly slow, but that's the point! Carefully copying each word and punctuation mark in a verse will give you a head start toward memorizing it. Just be sure to write the verse correctly! Early errors in memorizing are difficult to dislodge.

Scripture Memory Apps

Technology doesn't have to be a hindrance to your Scripture memory. In fact, there are numerous Scripture memory apps that streamline the process of memorizing and reviewing your verses. SMF's VerseLocker app is one of the most popular, and it's completely free. The app helps you memorize any verse of the Bible in the translation of your choice. If you're unsure about what to memorize, you can even download verse collections on topics like prayer, evangelism, hardship, and fear.

The best part of VerseLocker is that it simplifies the process of memorizing a verse. Tapping the "practice" button next to a memory verse opens up a variety of interactive memory tools. Visual learners can fill in the blanks with the correct words from their memory verse. Auditory learners can listen to their memory verses on a loop. You can track which verses you've memorized, schedule them for review, and even create shareable verse collections.

VerseLocker is available for free in the Apple, Google, and Amazon app stores. You can also use VerseLocker on your computer at verselocker.com.

Memory Palaces

Have you ever wondered how memory champions memorize the order of a deck of cards in only a couple minutes? No, they aren't prodigies with photographic memories. In fact, photographic memory is a myth. Sure, some people can memorize more efficiently than others, but we have no evidence of anyone ever possessing a truly photographic memory.[1] Instead, most experts use memory palaces to memorize things quickly, accurately, and lastingly.[2]

A memory palace is an imaginary room where you "store" the information you're memorizing. Usually, a memory palace is based on a place you visit often such as your home or office. As you memorize a passage of Scripture, you associate each phrase or verse with an object in the room. For example, here's one way to memorize Psalm 1:1 using your office as a memory palace:

> **"Blessed is the man who walks not"** Imagine a happy man standing on top of your desk.

> **"in the counsel of the wicked"** Imagine opening the top drawer of your desk and finding a letter filled with bad advice.

> **"nor stands in the way of sinners"** Imagine walking towards the door and leaping over a slippery pathway.

> **"nor sits in the seat of scoffers"** Imagine your chair filled with throat lozenges (a seat for coughers).

These may seem like crazy examples, but that's by design: unique, outlandish scenes are much easier to remember than a string of text. If you've already memorized the layout of your home, office, gym, or grocery store, you can start using the memory palace method right away with each part of

---

1 "Does Photographic Memory Exist?," Scientific American, Accessed May 30, 2023, https://www.scientificamerican.com/article/i-developed-what-appears-to-be-a-ph/.

2 Joshua Foer, *Moonwalking with Einstein: The Art and Science of Remembering Everything* (Penguin Books, 2011).

the room serving as an anchor for the text of your memory verses.

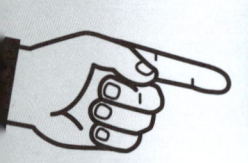

> ## "Memorization is the natural byproduct of repetition."

Creating a memory palace may seem unnecessarily complicated, but there's a reason it's the go-to method for most elite memorizers: it's incredibly effective once you get the hang of it.

💡 Learn more about using a memory palace to memorize Scripture at scripturememorypodcast.com/memorypalace.

Scripture Songs

Have you ever noticed that songs are much easier to memorize than Scripture? Most of us know the lyrics to dozens or even hundreds of our favorite songs. This is partially because music is rhythmic, poetic, and melodic. These factors, combined with the fact that music connects with our emotions, are what make it so easy to remember the words to your favorite songs. Plus, there's a good chance you've listened to your favorite songs hundreds of times over the years. As we've seen, memorization is the natural byproduct of repetition.

Scripture songs are a great way to harness the power of music as you memorize Scripture. If you're musically inclined, try composing your own Scripture songs. If you're not musical, use tunes you already know—even if that means recycling the tune to Amazing Grace! You can also visit scripturememory. com/songs to browse SMF's collection of word-for-word Scripture song albums.

Recite Aloud & Dramatically

I drive almost everywhere using GPS. This is convenient, but the disadvantage is that I can (and often do) drive somewhere a dozen times without remembering how to get there without my GPS. My memory shuts off as long as I know my phone will speak up when I need to make a turn.

Reading or listening to your memory verses can have the same effect. Of course, reading a verse is the first step toward memorizing it. But it's important to get your memory involved as quickly as possible. After reading the verse aloud 5-7 times, see how much you can say from memory. If you get stuck, reread the verse and find the next word or two. The goal at this stage isn't necessarily to recite perfectly; it's to "turn off the GPS" and see how far you can make it on your own.

It's also helpful to read and recite your memory passage dramatically. If you're memorizing a narrative passage, consider using a different voice for each speaker. If you're memorizing a psalm, try to express the psalmist's emotion in each verse. If you're memorizing an epistle, try emphasizing different words. These exercises will help you remember the meaning and message of your memory passage. Naturally, words are easier to remember when we understand their meaning.

> **"It's important to get your memory involved as quickly as possible."**

Memorize Using Initials and Acronyms

A popular way to memorize Scripture is by writing out the first letter of each word in your verse. "For God so loved the world" would be written as "F G s l t w."

Using a verse's initials to aid your memorization is somewhat like using training wheels on a bicycle: you shouldn't use them permanently, but they help you find your balance in the early stages of memorizing a passage.

For long lists of names (Rom. 16), virtues (1 Tim. 3), or vices (Rom. 1), try creating an acronym. For example, consider how you would learn the list of sins in Romans 1:29-30 "... envy, murder, strife, deceit, maliciousness. They are gossips, slanderers, haters of God, insolent, haughty, boastful...." This list could be memorized using the sentence, "Eventually My Sin Destroys My Gifts; Some Habits Incur Horrible Byproducts." Again, silly and vivid memory devices are often the most effective.

Tips for Memorizing Verse Numbers

It's true that God didn't inspire the chapter and verse numbers in your Bible. It wasn't until the Geneva Bible was published in 1560 that verse numbers became standard in our English Bibles. Being able to quote the precise words of Scripture accurately is much more important than knowing the exact chapter and verse. Even the author of Hebrews writes, "It has been testified *somewhere*, 'What is man, that you are mindful of him, or the son of man, that you care for him?'" (Heb. 2:6, emphasis added).

> **"Taking the extra time to learn the references is worthwhile."**

Even so, taking the extra time to learn the references is worthwhile. When you feel led to recite one of your memory verses to a friend, it's good to know precisely where that verse is found. Citing the reference does at least two things: it confirms that you're not making up these words, and it enables your listener to look things up for herself. To that end, take time to say the entire reference aloud every time you practice reciting a memory verse.

If you struggle to remember references, try looking for patterns in the verse numbers:

- Psalm 119:11 has a nine surrounded by ones.

- In Matthew 6:33, the sum of everything after the colon equals the chapter number (3 + 3 = 6).

- Romans 5:7 features consecutive prime numbers.

It's often even more helpful to associate the verse numbers with the text of the verse:

- If verse three talks about love, remember that you can draw a heart using the number three.

- If verse seven contains a key idea, remember that seven is a key biblical number.

- If verse 11 reintroduces an idea from earlier in the chapter, remember that the verse number is repetitive (two ones in a row).

- If verse 12 is lengthy, remember it has dozens of words.

- If verse 16 is particularly meaningful to you, remember "sweet 16."

- If verse 18 has instructions for spiritual maturity, remember that 18 is the legal age of adulthood.

Another method for memorizing verse numbers involves associating numbers with objects. A first-place trophy could represent the number one. Two could be represented by a pear, three by a tripod, and so on.

- When memorizing Psalm 1:1, imagine the man of God holding a first-place trophy.

"Don't underestimate the value of memorizing from a physical Bible."

- When memorizing Psalm 1:2, imagine him meditating on Scripture while eating a pear.

- When memorizing Psalm 1:3, imagine seeing a tripod stuck in the tree's branches.

The great thing about this method is that it's reusable. Once you associate an object with the number three, you can envision that object making an appearance anytime you're memorizing verse three of a chapter.

Keep a Notebook

Consider writing your memory verses in a pocket-size notebook and carrying it throughout the day. As you meditate on your verses, pull out your notebook anytime you forget which word comes next.

Use a Physical Bible

Don't underestimate the value of memorizing from a physical Bible—especially if you're a visual memorizer. Besides the fact that your Bible won't distract you with text messages and social media alerts, your paper Bible looks the same every time you open it. Verse 11 will always be waiting for you on the right-hand side of the page, about two inches from the bottom. Memorizing printed words on a tangible page is often easier than memorizing scrolling words on a backlit, cluttered screen. You can also personalize your physical Bible by underlining repeated words, circling verbs, highlighting favorite passages, etc. Wide-margin Bibles are especially well-suited for note-taking.

NOTES:

_____

_____

_____

_____

Chapter 5

> **Your word is a lamp to my feet and a light to my path.**
> **Psalm 119:105**

The scribes and Pharisees of Jesus' day could quote Scripture all day long. Still, they were "like whitewashed tombs, which outwardly appear beautiful, but within are full of dead people's bones and all uncleanness" (Matt. 23:27). How can we avoid a similar fate? For starters, begin your memorizing with a simple prayer: "Open my eyes, that I may behold wondrous things out of your law" (Psa. 119:18).

Knowing Scripture equips you to meditate on the Word of God "day and night" (Psa. 1:2). But if your memory verses never make the journey from your head to your heart, you haven't truly succeeded. "Blessed rather are those who hear the word of God and keep it!" (Luke 11:28). As you begin your study of a passage, take time to consider the following factors:[1]

The Historical Factor

Knowing the history behind your memory passage is a vital first step toward understanding its meaning. What was Paul's relationship with the Corinthians? Why was Daniel in Babylon? Why did Jesus' disciples want Him to overthrow the Roman empire?

Most study Bibles include brief Bible book introductions that answer these questions. Another helpful resource is bibleproject.com. Their short, animated videos cover the basics of each Bible book and highlight key historical factors that will enrich your Bible study.

---

1   Dr. Randy Williamson, Adapted from Dr. Ronald Meeks, *New Testament Survey I*, Blue Mountain College, August 2003.

The Literary Factor

Each book of the Bible can be classified by literary genre. Are you memorizing historical narrative, poetry, wisdom, prophecy, or an epistle? Answering this question will help you understand and apply God's Word correctly.

The Grammatical Factor

God didn't just inspire the ideas of Scripture; He inspired the very *words* of Scripture. As 2 Timothy 3:16 teaches, "All Scripture is breathed out by God."

The reason we memorize Scripture word-for-word is that "every word of God proves true" (Prov. 30:5). We see this in Matthew 22:23-32, where the Sadducees questioned Jesus regarding the resurrection. His response in verses 31-32 is particularly noteworthy: "And as for the resurrection of the dead, have you not read what was said to you by God: 'I am the God of Abraham, and the God of Isaac, and the God of Jacob'? He is not God of the dead, but of the living."

In His response, Christ quotes Exodus 3:6, emphasizing the phrase "I am" to demonstrate that God is *still* the God of Abraham, Isaac, and Jacob. Christ's argument rests on precise wording and even the tense of the verb! For us as well, considering the grammatical structure of a verse is an essential part of discovering its meaning.

The Contextual Factor

"Exegesis is the exposition or explanation of a text based on a careful, objective analysis. The word *exegesis* literally means 'to lead out of.' That means the interpreter is led to his conclusions by following the text."[2] Exegesis isn't about discovering what the Bible means to you; it's about discovering *what it really means*. Eisegesis, by contrast, is interpreting God's Word according to our preconceived ideas and biases.

2 "What is the difference between exegesis and eisegesis?," Got Questions, Accessed June 1, 2023, https://www.gotquestions.org/exegesis-eisegesis.html.

Invariably, this is what happens when we don't take time to study the context of our memory verses.

As you begin memorizing a passage, take time to consider its context. Where does the verse fit in the chapter? Where does the chapter fit in the book? Where does the book fit in the Bible? Knowing the answers to these questions will help you avoid the pitfalls of eisegesis. As the saying goes, "A verse without a context is a pretext."

The Spiritual Factor

"For whatever was written in former days was written for our instruction, that through endurance and through the encouragement of the Scriptures we might have hope" (Rom. 15:4). Once you've taken time to consider your passage's historical, literary, grammatical, and contextual factors, ask God to show you how its truth should shape your life.

What does your memory passage reveal about God? What does it say about man? Is there an example to follow, a command to obey, or a promise to remember? As we read in James 1:23-25,

> For if anyone is a hearer of the word and not a doer, he is like a man who looks intently at his natural face in a mirror. For he looks at himself and goes away and at once forgets what he was like. But the one who looks into the perfect law, the law of liberty, and perseveres, being no hearer who forgets but a doer who acts, he will be blessed in his doing.

Don't memorize Scripture to confirm everything you already believe about God. Instead, be prepared for the light of God's Word to refine your theology, convict your heart, and change your behavior.

"BUT WHAT IF I REALLY CAN'T MEMORIZE?"

Chapter 6

> Sanctify them in the truth; your word is truth.
> John 17:17

The human memory is incredibly powerful, yet one of the most common obstacles for would-be memorizers is the notion that they have a "bad memory." In chapter 1, we established that the human memory is very capable of memorizing Scripture; it's just that most of us have never (or barely) tried.

Before concluding that you have a bad memory, consider this remarkable assessment of the capacity of the human brain:

> *The human brain consists of about one billion neurons. Each neuron forms about 1,000 connections to other neurons, amounting to more than a trillion connections. If each neuron could only help store a single memory, running out of space would be a problem. You might have only a few gigabytes of storage space, similar to the space in an iPod or a USB flash drive. Yet neurons combine so that each one helps with many memories at a time, exponentially increasing the brain's memory storage capacity to something closer to around 2.5 petabytes (or a million gigabytes). For comparison, if your brain worked like a digital video recorder in a television, 2.5 petabytes would be enough to hold three million hours of TV shows. You would have to leave the TV running continuously for more than 300 years to use up all that storage.*[1]

This isn't describing the few and the gifted; it's describing you! The human brain is incredibly capable of memorizing

---

[1] "What Is the Memory Capacity of the Human Brain?," Scientific American, Accessed May 30, 2023, https://www.scientificamerican.com/article/what-is-the-memory-capacity/.

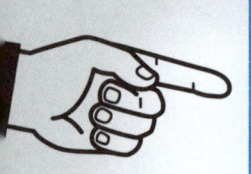

Scripture, even if it's unaccustomed to doing so. Before concluding that you truly have a bad memory, spend dedicated time every day memorizing Scripture using the methods described in this book. After a few months, you'll almost certainly discover that you *can* memorize Scripture.

Admittedly, there is a minority of people for whom this is not the case. Those suffering from various forms of cognitive impairment may find it especially difficult or even impossible to memorize. This raises a valid question: should we really bother memorizing Scripture if we are doomed to forget it? Why spend half an hour working on a verse you'll forget within a day? In his book *Keep In Memory*, Dr. N. A. Woychuk provides some helpful encouragement for those facing this dilemma:

> *I read about the man who complained to his pastor that he was much discouraged from memorizing the Scriptures in that he could not fasten anything in his memory that would remain. The elderly pastor had him take a pitcher, and fill it with water. When he had done it, he bade him empty it completely and wipe it clean so that nothing should remain of it. At that point the man wondered what was the meaning of it. "Now," said the pastor, "though there be nothing of the water remaining in it, yet the pitcher is cleaner than it was before. So, though your memory may seemingly retain nothing of the Word you memorize, yet your heart is cleaner because the Word went through it."*

> *About 20 years ago or so, a lady came to me after a service in east Texas and said, "I simply cannot remember anything, because my mind is like a sieve; the Word just runs through." "Keep*

memorizing the Word, Sister," I said, "it will keep your mind clean while it's running through." [2]

Time spent memorizing Scripture is never wasted. Even if you forget every verse you ever memorize, God's Word will purify your mind and life as it passes through. And don't forget: your memory will strengthen with use.

NOTES:

_____

_____

_____

_____

2 N. A. Woychuk, *Keep in Memory* (Scripture Memory Fellowship, 2020), 117-118.

Chapter 7 GETTING CHILDREN TO MEMORIZE SCRIPTURE

> I am reminded of your sincere faith, a faith that dwelt first in your grandmother Lois and your mother Eunice and now, I am sure, dwells in you as well.
> 2 Timothy 1:5

There's a reason you can still remember the songs, nursery rhymes, and TV shows of your childhood: children are incredibly good at memorizing. Consider the fact that most children are relatively fluent in their native language by just three or four years old. By age seven, they know their favorite dinosaurs' scientific names and behavioral patterns. At 10, they can explain the rules of baseball. At 12, they can often play their instrument better than adults who started playing in their twenties or thirties. When they learn a foreign language in their early years, they can speak it like a native, free of any foreign accent.

Clearly, God has given children a unique ability to memorize things quickly and lastingly. Unfortunately, most children lack the internal motivation to memorize Scripture. Adults often desire to memorize Scripture but find it difficult; children often find it easy to memorize but lack the desire.

When I speak at conferences and conventions, parents often visit SMF's booth of Scripture memory resources and pick out one of our family-oriented memory courses like *SwordGrip* or *14:6*. All too often, I've watched parents turn to their ten-year-old child and ask, "Is this something you would like to do?" When the child shrugs indifferently, the parent sighs, puts the book down, and longs for the day when her son or daughter will voluntarily begin memorizing Scripture.

Ironically, the same parents who let their children opt out of Scripture memory make other activities mandatory. Few children are eager to eat vegetables, do homework, complete household chores, go to bed on time, or brush their teeth. As long as children lack the internal motivation to do these things independently, parents proactively ensure they happen anyway. If you don't feel bad about requiring your children to brush their teeth, you shouldn't feel bad about requiring Scripture memorization. One prevents physical decay; the other prevents spiritual decay.

"But that's different. Scripture memory is a spiritual discipline. What if I force my kids to memorize Scripture and they grow up to hate the Bible?" Again, most Christian parents don't hesitate to make certain spiritual disciplines mandatory. Few children long to attend church on Sunday morning, but you bring them anyway. They don't see the need to bow their heads and give thanks before mealtime, yet you make them wait to eat until after the prayer. This isn't legalistic or abusive; it's good, biblical parenting. In the words of Solomon, "Train up a child in the way he should go; even when he is old he will not depart from it" (Prov. 22:6).

When parents let their children decide whether to memorize Scripture, it's usually because the parent views Scripture memory as the spiritual equivalent of an extra-curricular activity. We require them to apply themselves in math, but softball and chess club are optional. If our own perspective on Scripture memory is that it's more like soccer practice than science or history, we'll feel guilty about making it a requirement. On the other hand, when we are convinced with the psalmist that knowing God's Word by heart is of paramount importance (Psa. 119:11, 92), we'll stop at nothing to ensure it's written on the hearts of our children.

Of course, memorizing Scripture doesn't have to be as dreadful as a plateful of peas and broccoli. There are many ways to make Scripture memory a consistent and enjoyable part of your children's lives. Below are four tried-and-true ways to get your kids memorizing Scripture.

> **"Your way of memorizing Scripture will probably not resonate with your child."**

Make it rewarding.

Most Christian adults understand the value of knowing God's Word by heart. This awareness and some outside accountability (see chapter 2) are usually enough to keep them going. Since children typically lack the spiritual maturity to memorize on their own, look for creative ways to make it rewarding. Stickers, trophies, candy, or a family game night are often effective incentives. Charles Spurgeon's grandmother even paid him cash for every hymn he memorized as a child!

If this sounds like bribery, remember that our entire lives are based on the law of harvest: "whatever one sows, that will he also reap" (Gal. 6:7). As adults, this principle of labor and reward is what fuels every decision we make:

- We go to work to earn a paycheck, even when we'd rather sleep in.

- We mow our grass to have a nice lawn, even when we'd rather watch TV.

- We fill our cars with gas to avoid a breakdown, even when we'd rather go straight home.

Every day and all day, your decisions are based on the belief that the harvest will be worth the effort of planting. Rewarding children for memorizing Scripture may seem unspiritual, but it allows them to be motivated by the law of harvest when they are too young to appreciate the ultimate harvest that awaits them: the "good success" that comes from knowing and meditating on God's Word (Josh. 1:8). Scripture Memory Fellowship even offers an annual week of camp to children who memorize each year's theme verses.[1]

One parent said he would do anything that isn't sin to get God's Word into his children's hearts. That may sound extreme, but it's reasonable to offer external motivation until your child develops sufficient internal motivation. God's Word is more

---

1   More information at scripturememory.com/camp.

valuable than gold and sweeter than honey (Psa. 19), and children will learn this sweetness and value as they mature.

Make it fun.

Most children find adult habits and pursuits incredibly boring. Things like watching the news, folding laundry, and weeding the garden seem entirely unnecessary. Similarly, your way of memorizing Scripture will probably not resonate with your child. Your Scripture memory time may call for a quiet room with a stack of index cards, whereas your child might need games, Scripture songs, and hand motions. Below are several Scripture memory game ideas to help make Scripture memory enjoyable for kids.

Roll-a-Ball

Sit in the floor and roll a ball from person to person. The person who receives the ball says the next word or phrase in the verse before rolling it to someone else.

Whiteboard Relay

If you have four or more children, divide them into two teams. Place two whiteboards on the opposite end of the room. Much like a relay race, each team sends someone to the whiteboard to write the next word in the verse. The first team to finish the verse wins.

Word Shuffle

Write each word of the verse on a separate index card, mix them up, and see who can "reassemble" the verse fastest.

Verse Decoder

Prepare one note card for each of the verses your children have memorized. Write the reference on one side and the first letter of each word on the other. Show them the first letters and see who can provide the reference. Optionally, keep score and use a whiteboard instead of index cards.

Act It Out

Create hand motions or use sign language for each phrase in the memory verse. Most children also enjoy reciting the verse "in character." How would the verse sound if recited by a robot, superhero, newscaster, or Buggs Bunny?

Catch Me If You Can

Once your children know a verse fairly well, see if they can catch you making mistakes when you quote it. Of course, this presumes that you're memorizing with them.

Make it challenging.

As we've already seen, children are much better at memorizing than adults. Three verses per week might seem like a lot to most adults, but your child may be capable of achieving even greater results. So if you detect that your child can memorize his weekly verses with minimal effort, step it up a notch! You want to avoid making Scripture memory unreasonably difficult, but you also want to make "the best use of the time" while your children are uniquely capable of memorizing (Eph. 5:16). Ask God to give you wisdom in finding this balance.

Lead by example.

Suppose you required your children to eat vegetables and brush their teeth, but they never saw you do the same. They might submit to your parental authority, yet they would be much less likely to carry these habits into adulthood. The same is true of memorizing Scripture: if you aren't doing it, your children will notice and eventually follow suit.

All too often, Scripture memorization is viewed as a kids' activity that we relegate to Sunday School and Wednesday night children's programs. This means children often know God's Word better than we do. In Deuteronomy 6:5-9, God paints a very different picture of His design for families:

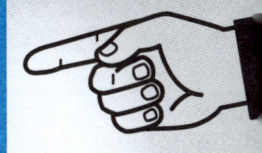

> **"The best way to convince your children that memorizing Scripture deserves to be a priority is by making it one yourself."**

> *You shall love the LORD your God with all your heart and with all your soul and with all your might. And these words that I command you today shall be on your heart. You shall teach them diligently to your children, and shall talk of them when you sit in your house, and when you walk by the way, and when you lie down, and when you rise. You shall bind them as a sign on your hand, and they shall be as frontlets between your eyes. You shall write them on the doorposts of your house and on your gates.*

In this passage, God calls parents to lead by example. Scripture must first be written on the hearts of the parents, who then teach it diligently to their children. Sadly, this model is often reversed. Too many of us are content to hear our children recite Scripture while giving ourselves a free pass. The best way to convince your children that memorizing Scripture deserves to be a priority is by making it one yourself.

NOTES:

_____

_____

_____

_____

Chapter 8 — WHEN MEMORIZING ISN'T FUN ANYMORE

> For the righteous falls seven times and rises again...
> Proverbs 24:16

Your zeal for God's Word was a bright flame that consumed your heart. But now, for some unexplainable reason, that flame has been reduced to an ember. The sad and simple truth is that you just don't feel like memorizing anymore.

It has been humorously observed that the definition of a godly husband is the man who keeps restarting family devotions. Similarly, you'll probably need to restart your Scripture memory routine from time to time. Sometimes your daily schedule will be disrupted by illness or out-of-town guests. Other times, you may find that Scripture memorization just isn't fun anymore.

When this happens, don't be discouraged. Generations of memorizers can relate to your struggle. Indeed, a desire to memorize that ebbs and flows is "common to man" (1 Cor. 10:13). When your desire to memorize Scripture needs rekindling, consider these helpful "fire starters."

- **Ask God for help.** If your heart needs a tune-up, look to the One who fashioned it (Psa. 33:15). Ask God to renew your appetite for His Word such that you can pray with Jeremiah, "Your words were found, and I ate them, and your words became to me a joy and the delight of my heart, for I am called by your name, O LORD, God of hosts" (Jer. 15:16).

- **Start with a clean slate.** Imagine if a runner missed a week of exercise and felt like he had to run 20 miles the next time he went to the gym. He would probably never go back! Similarly, if you miss a week or more of memorizing Scripture, it's usually best to start with a clean slate. Don't worry about how far behind you are. Instead, pick up where you left off and revise your target completion date if needed.

- **Memorize something else.** If you got bogged down on a difficult passage, set it aside for a few weeks and work on something more familiar. Memorizing a shorter passage or favorite psalm of 5-15 verses is a great way to get back on track and achieve an easy win.

- **Don't dread it.** The act of memorizing Scripture is usually more enjoyable than the thought of memorizing Scripture. You might spend all afternoon dreading the thought of rote memorization only to discover that your time in Scripture was the most refreshing part of your day. Once you finally get started, you might have a hard time stopping!

NOTES:

_____

_____

_____

_____

RESOURCES FROM SCRIPTURE MEMORY FELLOWSHIP

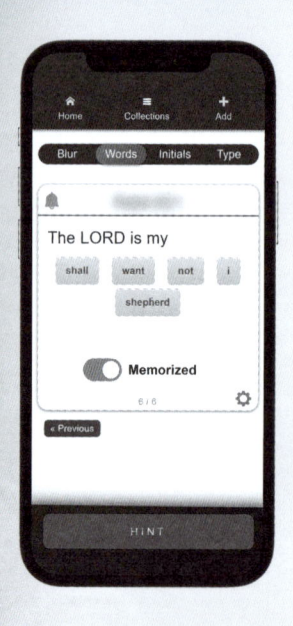

VerseLocker

Memorize any verse of the Bible in the translation of your choice with VerseLocker. Can you say your verse correctly as random words gradually disappear? If so, move on to the accuracy test and start typing your verse from memory. When you're done, see where you rank on the global leaderboard, organize your verses into custom collections, download sets of recommended memory verses, and listen as VerseLocker reads them aloud.

verselocker.com

The Scripture Memory Podcast

Memorizing Scripture will never come effortlessly, but we believe in making it as easy (and enjoyable) as possible. That's where The Scripture Memory Podcast comes in! Each episode features Scripture memory tips, techniques, and encouragement to help you stay on track in your Scripture memory journey. Podcast episodes are released twice a month, so be sure to subscribe to stay up to date.

scripturememory.com/podcast

The Classics

The Classics is a simple memory course of 100 key Bible verses everyone should know. These priceless passages of Scripture will be a continual source of strength, wisdom, and blessing in your walk with God. *The Classics* includes a memory booklet, perforated verse cards, and a verse card wallet.

scripturememory.com/classics

SwordGrip

SwordGrip is a comprehensive memorization plan that will familiarize you with Scripture from cover to cover. You'll learn key verses from every Bible book. The *SwordGrip* flipbook includes detachable verse cards, stickers to mark each week's recitation, and Grip-it-Tighter questions.

scripturememory.com/swordgrip

14:6

14:6 is a Scripture memory course that will help you embrace a biblical worldview in every area of life. The title is derived from the words of Jesus in John 14:6: "I am the way, and the truth, and the life." Each of the three volumes in *14:6* focuses on a different aspect of a biblical worldview.

scripturememory.com/146

Songs in the Night

Memorize 60 verses for hard times with five verses per week for 12 weeks. Whether it's your own trial or you're walking with a friend in a valley, knowing these verses by heart will be invaluable for the journey.

scripturememory.com/trials

Sermon on the Mount

Christ's Sermon on the Mount contains many famous passages, including the Beatitudes, the Lord's Prayer, and the wise and foolish builders. This memory journal helps you memorize all 111 verses of Matthew 5-7 in 23 weeks. Write out each verse in your favorite translation and answer the study questions to increase your understanding of God's Word.

scripturememory.com/mount

ABC Memory Book

The *ABC Memory Book* is our best and most popular memory book for preschoolers. Learn one verse of Scripture for each letter of the alphabet from A through Y, then read about the story of Zacchaeus for the letter Z. A short explanation, a related song or poem, and a beautiful watercolor illustration are included for every verse. This book is a great way to make Scripture a fundamental building block of your child's learning right along with the letters of the alphabet. The *ABC Memory Book* is also available as a musical CD or MP3 and as a coloring book.

scripturememory.com/abc

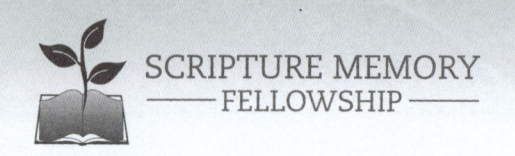

SCRIPTURE MEMORY
—— FELLOWSHIP ——

Who We Are

SMF exists to cultivate systematic Scripture memorizers who know Jesus Christ and grow in His likeness for the glory of God. We offer dozens of time-tested memory courses as well as a mobile app, Scripture songs, rewards, and more to equip memorizers of all ages to master the challenges of Scripture memory. We also host Scripture Memory Camp and ScriptureFests to help believers treasure the life-giving words of God. SMF operates primarily in the U.S. with ministry partners around the world.

Partner With Us

This ministry is a work of faith. Support from God's people allows us to continue operations and to offer Scripture memory materials at low cost.

God has faithfully supplied SMF's needs for decades through the sacrificial giving of His people. If you've been touched by our ministry and want to support this work of planting God's Word, please prayerfully consider giving (Rom. 15:27; 2 Cor. 9:7).